Trucks

Gail Saunders-Smith

Pebble Books

an imprint of Capstone Press

1

Pebble Books are published by Capstone Press
818 North Willow Street, Mankato, Minnesota 56001
http://www.capstone-press.com
Copyright © 1998 by Capstone Press

Library of Congress Cataloging-in-Publication Data
Saunders-Smith, Gail.
  Trucks/by Gail Saunders-Smith.
  p.cm.
  Includes bibliographical references and index.
  Summary: In simple text and photographs, describes a
variety of trucks and what they do, including garbage trucks,
cement mixers, snow plows, and mail trucks.
  ISBN 1-56065-496-1
  1. Trucks--Juvenile literature. [1. Trucks.] I. Title.

TL230.15.S28 1997
629.224--DC21
                              97-23582
                                 CIP
                                 AC

Editorial Credits
Lois Wallentine, editor; Timothy Halldin and James Franklin,
design; Michelle L. Norstad, photo research

Photo Credits
Unicorn Stock/H. H. Thomas, 6; Jeff Greenberg, 10; Florent
   Flipper, 18; Aneal Vohra, 20
Valan Photos/John Schakel Jr., cover; A.B. Joyce, 1, 16; Brian
   Atkinson, 4; B. N. Joyce, 8; J.A. Wilkinson, 12; Michael J.
   Johnson, 14

Table of Contents

Trucks carry logs.

Trucks haul garbage.

Trucks hold milk.

Trucks mix cement.

Trucks dump rocks.

Trucks plow snow.

Trucks lift people.

Trucks tow vehicles.

Trucks bring mail.

Words to Know

cement—a thick paste made from sand that becomes hard

dump—to empty

garbage—things people throw out

haul—to carry

plow—to remove or push aside

tow—to drag behind

truck—a large motor vehicle

vehicle—a car, truck, motorcycle, or tractor; people use vehicles to travel.

Read More

Marston, Hope Irvin. *Big Rigs.* New York: Dutton Cobblehill Books, 1993.

Ready, Dee. *Trucks.* Mankato, Minn.: Bridgestone Books, 1998.

Stephen, R. J. *The Picture World of Trucks.* Picture World. New York: Franklin Watts, 1989.

Internet Sites

Monster Truck's Home Page
http://www.geocities.com/MotorCity/5141

Truckworld Online!
http://truckworld.com/index.html

Monster Truck Racing Association
http://www.truckworld.com/mtra

Note to Parents and Teachers

This book describes and illustrates a variety of trucks and what they do. Each sentence includes a new verb and an object that helps identify the type of truck. The photographs clearly illustrate the text and support the child in making meaning from the words. Children may need assistance in using the Table of Contents, Words to Know, Read More, Internet Sites, and Index/Word List sections of the book.

Index/Word List

Word Count: 27
Early-Intervention Level: 3